AF480112

Wissahickon

Wissahickon

Poems

SCOTT ROBINSON

RESOURCE *Publications* · Eugene, Oregon

WISSAHICKON
Poems

Resource Publications
An Imprint of Wipf and Stock Publishers
199 W. 8th Ave., Suite 3
Eugene, OR 97401

www.wipfandstock.com

PAPERBACK ISBN: 979-8-3852-0380-2
HARDCOVER ISBN: 979-8-3852-0381-9
EBOOK ISBN: 979-8-3852-0382-6

10/24/23

Now the Wissahickon is of so remarkable a loveliness that, were it flowing in England, it would be the theme of every bard.

—Edgar Allen Poe

The Chief Elk replied, "You have wasted our flesh; desecrated our forest homes, and our bones; you have dishonored us and your-selves. We can live without you, but you cannot live without us!"

— Hìtakonanu'laxk[1]

Where we have failed to do
Aright, or wisely live,
Be warned by us, the better way pursue.

—Francis Daniel Pastorius, 1688

1. From "When the Animals Left," retold by Hìtakonanu'laxk in The Grandfathers Speak. Interlink Books, New York, 1994.

Contents

WISSAHICKON

Words and Things	1
Invocation	2
What Our Eyes Did	4
Stone Speaks	6
The Fox and the Goose	8
Jewelweed Speaks	9
White-tailed Deer Speaks	10
The Haunted Mill	11
The Fallen Tree	14
Golden Retriever Ponders the Impermanence of All Things	16
Gullywasher	17
The Maxims of the Trees	18
White Oak Speaks	19
Bitternut Hickory Speaks	21
The Light-bearer Speaks (American Holly)	22
Northern Pin Oak Speaks	23
American Beech Speaks	25
Honeycomb Coral Slime Mold Speaks	28
Creek Blessing	29
Cherry Blossoms	30
Hermit's Cave	31
Devil's Pool	34

Falling Off a Log   37
Crossing the Creek   38
the end   39

OTHER POEMS

The Truth from Below   43
If There Were No Such Thing as Food   44
Taliesin   45
Cleansing the Temple   49
Three Shelters   50
Coffee and Seroquel   51
Emrys Merddyn and the Two Dragons   52

Notes on the Poems   57

WORDS AND THINGS

Hungry are co-opting words, and lean,
That find a picture bright, and paint it duller.
Brave words of how Things are, and what they mean
Can fill the heart; Things-selves can fill it fuller.
In naming, we deplete things. Hearts are keen,
But cannot plumb the Spirit with a ruler.
Words limit. If we had no word for "green,"
The woods would be a reckless riot of color.

INVOCATION

"Split a piece of wood: I am there. Lift a stone, and you will find me there."

Gospel of Thomas, Saying 77b

Angels of the spirit of the fire,
     Angels of the spirit of the winds,
Angels of the spirit of the clouds,
     Angels of the darkness, and of snow,
Angels of the hail, and of the hoar frost,
     Angels of the thunder and the lightning,
Angels of the spirits of cold and heat,
     Of winter and of spring, autumn and summer
Angels of the trees and of the soil
     Angels of the rocks and of the waters
Angels of the birds and of the fishes
     And of all the spirits of all creatures
Which are in the heavens and on the earth,
     In the waters, and under the earth,

Remind me to observe, and to inquire
     Where every stream and ledge of rock begins,
Where white-tails browse, and screech-owls sound aloud
     Their eldritch cry; where geese bellow as though
Their young depended on it, and the cost
     Of silence, death. Whatever is enlightening
For me to see or hear, to mark or meet,
     Direct me to it; let me grow no numb-er

Than insufficient contact with the soil,
   And never having drunk of clean spring water
That wasn't pumped from wells with on/off switches
   Have already made me; and may my teachers
Be the fox and feldspar, and the girth
   Of fallen giant trees across the path.

Assist me now; my chronicle inspire;
   Where I can, help me to make amends
For the heedless blundering of crowds
   Who come, despoil, and, having plundered, go,
Leaving the new-found land more newly lost,
   Than ever it was before they found it; frightening
Every beast that went on hooves or feet,
   Birds and fish and insects without number;
Who dug for coal and pressed its smoking oil,
   Leaving to their sons and to their daughters
The bounty of the land, but not its wishes,
   Seeing nothing in the land but their own features,
Their house of mourning, and their house of mirth.
   A land of plenty, and the mind of dearth.

WHAT OUR EYES DID

The Wissahickon once had such a flow
That fifty mills made paper, oil, and cotton
Upon its banks. Today, most are forgotten,
The creek depleted, and its waters low.
Wissha mechan, the Lenapé people called it:
Catfish Creek. The large-mouth blues, and shad
That ran each spring, would make the channel dark,
A slippery mass of bodies, and men hauled it
Up to feed the tourists, who were glad
To feast upon the bounty of the park.

At dusk, the owls begin their hoots and screeching,
The deer come down to drink, the evening breeze
Draws whispered vespers from the leaves of trees,
A rasping forest chorus of beseeching
That alders, mountain maples, and black birches,
White ash, green ash, beech and birch and holly,
And sassafras and hemlock, serviceberry
And oak may be preserved from Man, who lurches
Into the woods, insensible with folly,
Whose eyes reduce the world to cash-and-carry.

There is a usefulness we cannot see
With eyes that take in, not what's there before,
But objects we can use to make us more—
Not Being, but Potentiality.

The shad no longer run, the blue catfish
Is gone, and neither mill nor turbine reap
The channel's force, the flow is so forsaken.
Yet even in depletion, though we wish
To bring the bounty back, the truth is deep:
There's bounty still, beyond what we have taken.

STONE SPEAKS

The Wissahickon Formation is. . .formed by very intense pressure upon. . .shales and sandstones; these were changed by metamorphism into schists and quartzites. . .The gneiss are composed of alternating bands of quartz, feldspar and mica.

–Guidebook to the Geology of the Philadelphia Area

You do not understand the soul of rock,
    neither do you comprehend the spirit of stone.
For whoever holds a garnet in the hand holds all garnet;
    for there is only one garnet, and each contains the whole in
    all its fullness;
Day and night it cries out, "We who are many are one body,
    for we all share in the one nature of garnet."
Pick up a stone; feel its heft, examine its many parts:
    granite and quartzite, feldspar and staurolite—
Yet it, too, cries out night and day, "We who are many are one
    body,
    for we all share in the one rock."
Even a rock of one stuff, like limestone,
    precipitated out of solution,
Formed into stone by eons of heat,
    pressed into rock by ages of pressure,
    cries out morning and evening:
"Come, seek out my caves and my fossils,
    brave my lakes and my drumlins;
"For we are one in the nature of calcite,
    and one in the body of this rock."

Therefore, think less of a chiseled soul, with boundaries and a shape,
  and more of a flow of spirit,
Ever recombinant, ever here at hand;
  ever crystalizing, ever omnipresent.

THE FOX AND THE GOOSE

I saw a white goose from across the creek.
She's built her nest too near the path, I thought.
A moment's waiting down the dirt trail brought
A fox, who, startled, froze there, looking meek
As the wombed demon snaked her coiling neck
And, scant inches from his toothy mug, hissed
Her terrifying warning. Fox missed just
A beat before he turned attention back
To business, trotting coolly through the schist,
Clearly seeing no reason for a fuss.

The target of the Fury's ward-spell grim,
His arrogance was studied, not unruly,
His tail held high, not hurrying unduly—
No mother goose would get the best of him!
"What goose?," his trot implied; "I haven't seen
A thing! Nobody here to scare a beast
Of legendary cunning and resource."
The goose went back to sitting, ever keen
To scare the daylights out of those who feast
On gosling—or who even come too close.

JEWELWEED SPEAKS

The little jewelweed sprouts from the fallen tree
That hasn't even finished turning back into dirt yet,
Such a juggernaut is its date with life.

We need to stop mewling and yammering about "destroying the
　earth."
The earth will bury us all.
We need to get comfortable with "destroying ourselves,"

Which is what we actually mean, banging on about "destroying the
　earth."
"Don't get too big for your britches,"
Says the little jewelweed.

WHITE-TAILED DEER SPEAKS

I see you from up here, your dog worrying
That naked young skull of one of my kind.
There's no meat on it, the eye sockets blind,
But there's thick scrub between us; I'm not hurrying
Away. Whatever will you do with that?
For that, what would we do with one of yours?
Come to think of it, here in the out-of-doors,
We never cross a corpse of you. Why's that?
What happens? Do you crumble into dust?
Or go back where you came here from, from some
Far Elsewhere, where the things you need don't come
Without a fight? We often think you must.
I've seen yours buried; isn't that a waste?
Can't even crows and foxes have a taste?

THE HAUNTED MILL

Unless you repent, you too will all perish. (Luke 13:3)

We no longer pour blood on the foundations,
Believing we have outgrown sacrifice.
But a creek-side cotton-house's conflagrations
Relayed the urgent warnings of John Wise.

So this is how it happened: old John Gorgas
Had built twin grist mills on the Oil Mill Run,
With matched adjoining vineyards. Soon, the millrace
Turned shafts as grapes hung ripening in the sun.

The wheels turned, and the years turned; a new century
Saw John Wise in possession of the first
Of Gorgas' mills, and with this business venture, he
Stepped up to slake the sacrificial thirst.

On one fine day that seemed like any other,
Wise was inspecting drive shafts in the mill;
He leaned in for a closer look, and Mother
Nature moved in swiftly for the kill.

The cogs that transferred power from the millrace
Into the wallowers that cranked the stone
Crushed Wise's head between them, and his old face
Poured down like wine. The creek had claimed its own.

But Wise's blood was not, itself, sufficient
Offering to appease the injured land;
But with the cotton mill came an efficient
Way for Wise's ghost to take his stand.

John Gorgas Jr. built a mill extracting
Oil from wool—gave Oil Mill Run its name.
It was retooled for making cotton wadding,
Through which Wise sent communiqués of flame.

The bone-dry cotton-house the spirit beckons,
Who, with a gesture, sets a bale alight.
A fireball engulfs the whole in seconds,
And into lurid day transforms the night.

Again, again he sent his fiery warning;
The dry-house fires numbered thirty-five;
The mill itself burned eight times, till the morning
They gave it up in 1885.

The mills have gone away, the catfish also;
The public fountains no more safe to drink;
A few mill dams still make small waterfalls, so,
"How picturesque!" the happy tourists think.

The streams are shrunk, the channels torn and shaken;
The shad are gone, and it's too late to rue it.
This isn't free, and payment will be taken,
Beyond John Wise's cerebrospinal fluid.

But we don't like to think about the reckoning,
The bill that comes inexorably due;
Not when distractions of all kinds are beckoning,
And prophets speaking truth to power are few.

Eat, drink, and merry be while we are able;
It's not just Rome—the whole green world's afire;
Regard the Arizona water table,
In case you think the prospect isn't dire.

For *Dies irae, dies illa solvet*
Saeclum in favilla, goes the chant
That hymns the end of everything. Revolve it
In your mind before you say we can't

Do anything about it. Earth will rise up,
And mortals everywhere will stand aghast,
Raising heaven-beseeching hands and eyes up—
And earth will have her sacrifice at last.

THE FALLEN TREE

A big tree fell across the creek, its roots
A mid-air mandala, a sacred space
Of spreading limbs and filaments, a place
To hide oneself from all the daily brutes
Who tromp, big-booted, over things of grace—
Who mock enchantment. When I was a kid,
I found just such a refuge in the wood.
Hidden from the path, there I could brace
Myself with solitude, and there I fled
And hid myself, and found that I was good.

I sat with my own thoughts, the living woodland
Took me in and gave me back myself—
A thing of wonder, me, escaped by stealth,
With, briefly, the enchantments close at hand.
And like the shrubs around, I grew apace,
Then sought enchantments elsewhere. Still, I took
My new friends with me to my childhood bunker.
Tales of Galadriel, and of the place
Called Avalon, where once a boy who shook
The world was laid, whence he'd return in wonder.

I read The Trojan Women there: *Here lies*
A little child, slaughtered by the Greeks
Because they were afraid. Euripides
I loved, because he snuck me prurient peeks
Into the rank corruption of the whole.

And Aeskylos! The atavistic sage,
Who trafficked in raw savagery, outrage,
And horror, slaking my suburban soul.
Then I discovered Ireland; page by page
Devouring Yeats, the man who would be mage.

Splendid old pagan! I climbed Queen Maeve's cairn,
And saw the dolmens, standing stones, and mounds.
I bought a pennywhistle, made the rounds,
Immersed myself in jigs and reels and airs—
The tunes of wonder—till I got so good
That folk would listen when I sang and played;
I reveled in the magic close at hand.
But by that time I was in different woods,
And it was business; I was getting paid,
Making CDs, performing with a band.

I haven't had an isolated place,
Sacred to the enchantments, since I shaved,
And walked into the day-to-day, and braved
A world that wasn't stillness, but a race.
I could come here! I could be apart—
A lonely, landlocked salmon of an elf;
But I have clothes to wash, supper to eke
Out, and a dog to walk. When did my heart
Forget to let the woods give me myself?
What am I searching for beside the creek?

GOLDEN RETRIEVER PONDERS THE IMPERMANENCE OF ALL THINGS

Well, yeah, these are the same woods that I ran
In all the time, but, everything is new!
For instance, though the sticks still smell like you
When I retrieve 'em, everything on land
Smells different. And because I'm a good dog,
When you say Sit, I sit—but you should know:
Nothin' for really ever stops; it's Go,
Go, Go for every animal and log
And rock and bird—they don't stay for a minute!
That's why I run around and sniff at stuff;
My nose is never full—never enough!
Even the creek has different dead stuff in it.
So if you're asking, that is my advice:
You can't retrieve sticks in the same creek twice.

GULLYWASHER

Everything green rejoices,
Everything brown gives thanks;
All the streams raise their voices,
Rushing to flood their banks.

The wind whips the trees; skies blacken,
Temperatures drop like a stone;
Nor will the downpour slacken
Until its work is done.

THE MAXIMS OF THE TREES

Leaving my Dad-and-his-Demons apartment, a.k.a. my Assisted Living Bullpen, a.k.a. The White Dog Hermitage, I took up my trekking pole and headed to the woods to gather the maxims of the trees. The summer morning was mild, and I decided to head into the bottomlands first, so as to leave them before the mosquitos got too bad, and emerge onto high ground before it began getting dark.

At the top of the rise, I met a majestic White Oak: eighty feet tall and another eighty feet at the crown. What such a commanding old tree, source of food to over 500 creatures, could tell me, I was eager to find out.

"What news?" I asked. The venerable tree replied:

WHITE OAK SPEAKS

Eldest am I in this place,
And I can see very far:
Each creature in its own place,
Working to stay what they are.

You think there are objects at rest?
I tell you: immutable law
Decrees that each one do its best
At working to stay what they are.

Not a thing lasts, yet duration
And labor make real every flower;
No creatures in all of creation
But are working to stay what they are.

Thanking the tree for its wisdom, I began the steep descent toward Cresheim Creek.

The soil became damper as I went, and sandier. At a place where private homes backed onto the top of the gorge, a cobble-stone-lined drainage channel crossed the path; empty now, it was presumably for carrying storm-water from someone's yard into the creek.

I started at the sight of it; it reminded me of a channel that drains the Japanese Garden into the Swan Pond at the Morris Arboretum. When my elder daughter was still in diapers, she would always toddle into the channel and touch the palms of her hands to the cobbles, filling her diaper to bursting with water as she reached down. Bottomlands, indeed!

We had so many songs, my little girls and I: table-grace songs, bathtub songs, changing-table songs. One day, as we pulled out of the arboretum parking lot, my elder daughter said, "Sing adobetum, Daddy!" So I sang arboretum off the top of my head. We all still know the song. God, I miss those days.

All this I thought in the time it took to step over the cobbled drainage channel.

I met a Bitternut Hickory on a tiny island in the middle of the creek. Seeing the clusters of little round nuts, with their paper-like, dusty-yellow coverings like Japanese lanterns, I made a mental note to come back in the fall to see its spectacular gold-yellow foliage.

Hailing it as I approached, I asked what it had to say. It said,

BITTERNUT HICKORY SPEAKS

I grow where the soil
Is poor and wet. Destiny
Has decreed my part.
If you seek sweet mast, do not
Look to me; I am busy.

In her autobiography, St. Terésa of Avila wrote,

> *Christ has no body now but mine. He prays in me, works in me, looks through my eyes, speaks through my words, works through my hands, walks with my feet and loves with my heart.*[1]

In my most recollected moments, when I really have my spiritual wits about me, I remember to "invite Jesus into my eyes"—to consciously offer my eyes for Jesus' use. I do this in crowds, at protest marches, in shopping malls, and among the poor and unsheltered, and the more I do it, the easier I believe it becomes to see others as God sees them.

I also do this in the woods. I'm sure Jesus never saw woods like mine with his earthly eyes, so I invite him into my eyes and offer up to him the adventure of seeing. The Bhagavad Gita calls this "offering up the objects of sense perception in the fire of the senses." (4:26)

The path ascended until the soil was well-drained, and, in the partial-to-full shade, I found a stand of hollies. As I gazed in wonder at the richly deep-green leaves, I heard the voice of the largest, oldest holly ringing through my head.

---

1. Terésa of Avila, *Life of Teresa of Jesus*

THE LIGHT-BEARER SPEAKS (AMERICAN HOLLY)

"Lucifer" means "one who bears the Light."
Take me into your home when all is dark,
And frosts of winter leave their leafy mark
On window-panes. My leaves and berries bright
Will shine Midsummer into every heart
That falters when the sun is low and dim.
The old Oak King—I wrest his power from him
At Midsummer. From then I do my part
To hold the light throughout the months when light
Is precious; to hold warmth when days are cold.
Green leaves and blood-red berries make a bold,
Hale welcome to the Yule, that sets aright
The year which, taking rest in the declining,
Awakens to the newborn sun's first shining.

Holly thrives in acidic soil, and sure enough, I found nearby the squat little acorns of the Northern Pin Oak, with their caps covering half the nut or more. The Pin Oak makes the soil around it acidic. In gratitude for nurturing the hollies, I saluted the tall, old tree.

NORTHERN PIN OAK SPEAKS

You deplore
My acorns are too small and bitter, so you just ignore;
You're blue
Because the cap-to-nut ratio is simply not worth it to you.
You're in need,
But remember how you turned up your noses in finicky greed?
Now I can laugh,
Knowing you would return after taking that bath.

You'll be back, in the snow,
When your food supply is running low,
And your lives won't be lost
If you're able to dig through the frost.
Snowdrifts rise, acorns fall
And my canopy is just as tall
As the oaks you admire
And you'll have to come back groveling to get the nourishment
  you require!

You'll be back, never fear,
To eke out your straitened rations here;
I will feed you once more,
When there's nothing on the forest floor.
When they're gone, my acorns,
You can greet the spring and toss your horns,
For when push comes to shove

You will choke those bitter acorns down to remind me of your
  love.

At the top of a rise, where the east bank of the Cresheim
Creek trail veers away from the stream toward one of the only two
pine-forested areas in the park, I saw a spindly beech sapling, no
more than three feet tall, clinging to a level place in the mostly
shady spot. Once, I would have thought it a Johnny-come-lately,
showing up a day late and a dollar short to establish itself amongst
the fully-grown trees that surrounded it. But when I learned about
forest succession, I realized the opposite was the case—this sun-
starved little relic of a species that *starts* forests had hung on past
its usefulness among other trees that, as dominant as they are now,
wouldn't have been able establish themselves had the trail not been
blazed by the beeches, birches, and other early-growth trees. I felt,
keenly, its pain.

AMERICAN BEECH SPEAKS

When a forest burns down, or is clear-cut,
My kindred and I are the first
To put down deep roots from the beech-nut,
To thrive where conditions are worst
For the tulip poplars that follow,
And the hemlock and oak in their turn;
And when they are thriving, it's hollow
And spent I become. Let it burn.

Back in the early 90's, I made an unsuccessful run at the ordained ministry in the Episcopal Church. (No, let's not say "unsuccessful"; let's just say I didn't make it through The Process, for better or worse.) I was living in conservative Lancaster at the time, and, noticing the large community of Pagans there, I suggested the Diocese host a Christian/Pagan Day of Dialogue. Not long after, the priest supervising my pastoral internship got a letter from the bishop saying he would not support my going forward in The Process. Stapled to the letter was the sample flyer I had made for the event.

Now, attitudes are relaxed, and some dinosaurs slouching toward the Great Tar Pit in the Sky. A younger colleague of mine made it through The Process and was ordained while an initiated Sufi; I have heard people gush about how he taught them to dervish-whirl at some retreat or other. And I don't begrudge him his ordination; he is a smart, energetic, big-hearted servant of God, and we are blessed to have him. But I do feel a little like a spindly beech tree sometimes, watching the younger, tougher trees take root and thrive.

Many Episcopal churches now invite to the table, not merely "all baptized Christians," but "everyone without exception." Hearts, minds, doors are opening, inside and out. When I try to put my experience with Parkinson's to good use for the benefit of others, I feel the Spirit of Christ moving in me. When I see my dog barreling down the greening path in the springtime woods, I feel the Green Man all around me. The day of dialogue is happening at last, inside me. And it's beautiful.

I hiked with my dog along the Wissahickon, north of the Bells Mill Road Bridge. The path is flat there, and close to the water, making it ideal for throwing in sticks for him to retrieve. I picked my way carefully amongst the rocks, shoulders hunched with Parkinson's, grumpy about the rain that had just started to fall, and simply not feeling it. Realizing that time spent like this was time wasted, even in the woods, I remembered the Seven Elements Meditation.

Facing east, I focused my attention on the element of Air, becoming aware of the faint, cool breeze from the south upon my right cheek. Turning south, I brought my attention to the element of Fire. Sometimes I do this by visualizing a campfire, or the invisible jet of flame shooting from the glory hole into which my friend the glassblower inserts blobs of melted rock on the end of a blowpipe. Most often, though, I become conscious of the currents of life-energy pulsing through my breath and heartbeat, the fire of respiration powering the engine of life. My pulse quickens and my breathing accelerates as I feel and remember, *I am not dead yet.*

I then turned west to contemplate Water—easy enough to do with the creek to the west of the trail. The sound of flowing water is my favorite sound, so I listened for a long time with eyes closed before opening them to watch the running current. Turning to the north, I focused on the element of Earth, gazing at the great gray boulders and silvery slabs of Wissahickon schist all around me.

There are additional operations for energies above, below, and within, but my dog was growing restless, so I omitted them this time. I walked away energized, recollected (as the Christian

mystics say) and much more present to my surroundings than be-
fore. Whatever path you follow, if it includes a way to touch in with
the here and now, I commend it to you.

Fall is coming on; the first leather-glove-brown leaves are
beginning to accumulate on the sidewalks. But in the woods, it's
still late summer. Passing a fallen tree that someone had splashed
brilliant white paint on, I heard a voice:
"Hey, stupid!" I looked around for the source of the greeting.
"Yeah, you—the tourist with the dog!" The voice, weirdly,
seemed to be coming from the splash of white paint. "You want
maxims?" it said. "Oh, I'll give you maxims!"

HONEYCOMB CORAL SLIME MOLD SPEAKS

The trees get all the attention—
"How lovely the foliage of fall!"
We fungi get honorable mention
If we get any kudos at all.

But the slime molds in glittering purple,
In orange and yellow and pink,
In familiar mold forms, and a couple
Unlike anything you could think,

Are already bursting with colors
You'll never see anywhere else;
And the humble trametes, while duller,
Is almost as white as myself.

In pursuit of the bright hues autumnal,
Some people will drive pretty far;
But to bask in the colors we've got—well,
They'll just have to get out of the car.

It is winter. I believe I will gather no more maxims for now.

Walk the winter woods.
See: moss greening on the rocks
In living water.

CREEK BLESSING

I found the stones beside the Cresheim Creek
And Wissahickon, took them home and blessed
Them with creek water, leaving them to rest
Till Winter Solstice. Middle of the week
It was, a Wednesday morning; none could bear
Us company, my dog and me, so forth
We went, and by the East, West, South, and North,
Asked blessings on the currents with a prayer.
I left the stones beside the streams, to leach
Their benedictions in the frost-kissed brooks,
And clambered up the bank, and made for home.
I did no exegesis, didn't preach,
But hauled my face out of my many books,
And waters, gorges, trees were all my tome.

CHERRY BLOSSOMS

It might have come straight from a Lovecraft tale,
This color out of space, above the new
Pale, hopeful breath of greening, as the dew
Endamped the undergrowth. High over all,
The cloud of pink, as through the smoke of grapeshot
Flashed out, and hovered in the evening air,
Surprising as an ostrich over there,
A thing all unprepared-for by my thought.
This ornamental in the birthing wood
Seemed out of step, like something markered in
By chubby, sticky hands. This place is thin.
Pink blossoms, pale green leaves, black sticky mud,
A cotton-candy-colored flag unfurled;
An emissary from another world.

HERMIT'S CAVE

You bid us believe in the Creator and Preserver of Heaven and Earth, though you do not believe in Him yourself, nor trust in Him. For you have now made your own the land we held in common amongst ourselves and our friends. You now take heed, night and day, how may you keep it, so that no one may take it from you. Indeed, you are anxious even beyond your span of life, and divide it among your children, this manor for this child, that manor for that child. But we have faith in God the Creator and Preserver of Heaven and Earth. . .and we believe and are sure that He will also preserve our children after us, and provide for them, and because we believe this, we bequeath them not a foot of land.

–A Lenapé elder to William Penn, as recorded by Johannes Kelpius

Even the guidebooks say you lived here,
    the tourist pamphlets that you spent your days
In this damp hole in the earth,
    this man-made cave.
The Rosicrucians raised a plaque outside the door,
    a monument between the path and cave,
Proclaiming you were one of them,
    declaring your faith in their gnostic sect.
Your teacher Boehm would have laughed in their faces,
    the shoemaker sage have held them in derision,
And you, yourself, have perished in the cave,
    shaken by agues in that stone-lined cell
Had you attempted to dwell there,
    instead of just retreating to it for meditation,
    so chancy was your health.

I leash my dog to a tree outside the door—
    no power on earth can coax him into entering—
Lighting incense until the smoke pours through the portal
    as from a slumbering dragon on a hoard;
I try to cleanse the hole with myrrh and prayer,
    to purify it with burnt offering and petition.

What made you think you would find her here,
    the woman in the wilderness revealed to Saint John?
She cried out in the pangs of labor,
    writhed in her birth-agony
As the red dragon waited to devour the child she would bear,
    the ancient serpent to gulp down her son.
But God snatched her son away to safety,
    and led his mother to the wilderness, away from the devourer.

You built cells for your monks,
    raised up a school for your neighbors' children;
You fashioned an infirmary to cure their ills,
    a dispensary for herbs your gardens gave,
    the leaves of the trees for the healing of the nations.
You also planted herbs to help you see
    the woman who, you thought, was in these woods,
    biding her time until the dragon was cast down.
How many nights did you look for her from the tower,
    those long dark nights of watching in the woods?
Did your pharmacopeia open your eyes to visions,
    your herbs show you signs in the night?

You thought the peoples here the lost tribes of Israel,
    these forest folk the ten tribes gone astray,
And so, you came like Israel, building homes and inhabiting them,
    planting vineyards and eating of their fruit.
You believed you would see with your own eyes the dissolution of
    all things,
    hear with your own ears the final trumpet's blast.
The appointed time came and went,
    the day of doom failed to appear.
You died, and your people were dispersed;
    you perished, and they went to Ephrata
To join the disciples of Conrad Beissel,
    to await the Kingdom with the baker sage.

How is it that you tried to build a lasting city in the gorge,
    to raise up fences in the primal woods,
when you yourself heard the Lenapé elder say—
    took down the words he spoke to William Penn—
that people trust in God who raise no fences,
    that deeds and titles are for those who have no faith?

DEVIL'S POOL

Three young men went down to Wissha Mechan —
   a hot day it was, and the sun beating down—
to cool themselves in the current,
   to swim away sweat and sunburn.

Matantu, the grim spirit, spied on their approach,
   the dweller in the deeps watched their coming;
From his place in Devil's Pool he beheld them:
   three young men, and one a head taller than his fellows.
This man-boy, he thought, the slim-but-wiry,
   will be a fine mate for my daughter,
In the swift deeps of Ganshowahanna,
   in the cold deeps of the roaring river.
I will send her forth in a swift current,
   in a deadly cresting I will dispatch her,
To sweep away the lofty one,
   to drag him to the depths to be her man.

The boys entered the creek, splashing in the shallows,
   the young men dove into the current where it deepened;
Without warning, a wall of water roared down the gorge,
   a mighty surge overwhelmed them,
Sweeping away the tall one,
   dragging down their companion.

Later, the two described a woman—
    like a water spirit she appeared to them,
Fierce to drag away their fellow,
    pitiless to pull him under.

The boy's parents mourned for him,
    father and mother lamented his loss.
Without even a body to bury,
    mortal flesh to commit to the earth,
Hope grew like skunk cabbage in the bottoms,
    like mushrooms it took root within them.

In a forest clearing nearby lived a shaman;
    only a few miles off he made his home.
A Lenapé-Shawnee half-blood he was—
    —for the Shawnee were friends to the Lenapé-wak—
Skilled to consult departed spirits,
    practiced in communing with the dead.
They took whiskey and tobacco to the seer,
    with liquor and Lënii kshatay they plied him,
Beseeching him to say if their boy still lived,
    to set their anxious minds at rest.
Come back in two days, he told them,
    and I will give you an answer.

The seer withdrew deep into the forest,
    beneath a white oak he drank and smoked,
Until the Chipe-wak gathered around him,
    the spirits of the departed whispered in his ears.

Your boy is alive, he informed the mourners,
  you will see him, and your hearts will be at rest.
*Let the people come to the confluence of the Gonshowahanna and
  the Lenapéwihittuk,*
  *let them gather where the Roaring River and the River of the Lenapé
  meet.*

By dawn the people were assembled,
  and when the morning mist burned off, they saw a wonder:
Lightning flashed, the thunder-beings roared,
  whirlpools churned in the current;
They saw the man-boy rise from the river—
  beheld him alive and well, standing in the Lenapéwihittuk.
As they watched, they saw a young woman appear,
  in human form, yet like a manëtu,
Standing beside the youth of the Lenapé-wak,
  the living child of the people with the child of Matantu.

For a long time the people watched the two,
  and when they had seen, their spirits were at rest.
Alive was the boy in the heart of the river;
  The lost one was seen, and was found.
When the people had gazed their fill,
  man-boy and spirit-woman vanished from their sight.
The people went home rejoicing,
  light of spirit walked the Lenapé-wak—
For a man of the people lived in the river's heart,
  and the depths of the river in the hearts of the people.

FALLING OFF A LOG

I'd had brain surgery two days before
I took my dog out hiking in the wood.
The doctors told me walking was as good
An exercise as any—and what's more,
It wouldn't put my head beneath my heart.
Om mane padme hum I used to chant—
"The jewel is in the lotus"—but you can't
Scoop dog poop off the grass until you start
To see: your head must humbly race the heart
To earth. Back in the woods, I sat to rest
Upon a fallen tree so soft with dew
And rot, it bent beneath my weight, and art
And grace and dignity and I slid west,
And fell into a bush. And then I knew.

CROSSING THE CREEK

Right through the center of the channel runs
A current in the creek so powerful
That though my dog charge through it like a bull,
He's swept downstream en route. He turns and guns
His way to the back-eddy, where I threw
A stick, that, slow and stationary, turns
As leisurely as Bacchus on an urn,
Until he grasps the prize, intent to chew
For all he's worth. Back through the channel then
He fights his way, through current now reversed.
This is a process he has long rehearsed—
Crossed over for the stick, and crossed again.
However powerful the stream may be,
The goal awaits in all tranquility.

THE END

there is stillness, and
there is motion, but never
just, until the end.

Other Poems

THE TRUTH FROM BELOW

When Wisdom made the galaxies,
And then was born on Mary's knees,
Then Joseph wiped the blood away,
And wrapped placenta in the hay.

From fashioning the furthest star,
Love came to join us as we are;
Took on a body—dust and clay—
In the accustomed, messy way.

Why, then, did the Apostle say,
To us who celebrate today
And gaze in wonder at the crèche,
"Make no provision for the flesh"?

IF THERE WERE NO SUCH THING AS FOOD

If there were no such thing as food, my flesh
Would not be hungry. If there were no song,
I wouldn't need to sing, nor would I long
For love, if love were not, to come refresh
My aching, desert heart. We do not want
For things that don't exist—though I have known,
My whole life long, a craving to return,
A homesickness for where I'd be, but can't
Identify. I think it must be God.
And though I love the earth beneath my feet,
There's something unfulfilled and incomplete
In every path my restless soles have trod.
There must be soul-food somewhere, dressed and carved;
My belly full, my soul forever starved.

TALIESIN[2]

Ceridwen was mistress fair of poetry and song;
She had two children with her mate, a giant grim and strong.
Her daughter was the loveliest the land had ever seen.
Her son was hideous, ugly, grossly stupid, coarse and mean.

Ceridwen brewed cauldron after cauldron full of spells
To heal her son's obscenity. She begged the holy wells
To fill her cauldron one last time, a towering spell to cast;
She gathered herbs, intoned the words, till all was primed at last.

When spell was ripe, then three mere drops would change the
    gnarled young man
Into a Bard with insight, words, and magic at command,
Skill in poetry and song, and gifts of prophecy;
In one year's time, her son would be reborn a prodigy!

But only those three drops would work that left the cauldron first;
The rest would turn to poison, and the land become accursed.
She would not let that happen, swore the Lady Ceridwen,
And the Fae themselves would notice take of her High Bardic son.

Gwion Bach, a servant boy, was set to stir the brew;
A blind man piled on the wood to feed the flames anew;
A year, a day, from sundown to sunrise, must Gwion stir;
The fire must not go out, the stirring paddle never tire.

2. Semi-legendary 6th-century CE Welsh bard.

The year and day were passed away, and Gwion, growing weary,
Was careless with the paddle as his eyes grew dull and bleary.
Three drops leaped from the cauldron to his thumb; without a
    thought
He thrust the thumb into his mouth because the drops were hot.

Gwion felt the change in mind and body with the brew,
And in her great hall, Ceridwen felt also, and she knew.
"The slave has stolen the saving drops were meant to heal my son!"
Gwion turned into a hare and over the fields did run.

Into a greyhound Ceridwen transformed herself, and ran;
Gwion saw her coming, to a salmon changed, and swam.
She turned herself to otter bitch to pull him from his skin;
He turned into a swallow—the air-currents he would skim.

She changed into a hawk, and he, spying a heap of grain,
Changed into one, sole kernel, never to be found again.
So wroth was Lady Ceridwen for her benighted son,
She changed into a giant hen, and ate them, every one.

The cauldron cracked, and spread its poison all throughout the land;
It fouled the drinking water; men with horses at command
Found corpses where their beasts had drunk, because the Lady's
    brewing
Killed fish and bird and beast and man, and left all things in ruin.

Before six weeks were past and gone, she knew she went with child;
Moreover, she knew who it was; the knowledge drove her wild.
For Gwion Bach grew strong within, waiting to be reborn.
She vowed to kill him when his eyes first opened on the morn.

But babe within and babe without are not the same, she learned;
She beheld her child's beauty, and she could not have him burned.
She set him in a coracle and let him drift away.
He fetched up on a salmon weir just at the break of day.

The man who pulled him out looked not for anything amazing;
He beheld the child's radiant brow, and murmured, *"tal iesin!"*[3]
And that became his name; his fame spread like a flame around;
His prophesies and poems led kings to victories and crowns.

He's known as greatest of Welsh bards, for poetry and magic,
For prophecy and song that hymned triumphant things and tragic.
He brought good fortune to the kings of Britons and of Welsh,
And all because he tasted brew was meant for someone else.

<u>Epilogue</u>
To brew a brew that would *all* renew—it's really almost funny;
For brotherly love's for brotherly love, but medicine's for money.
And if the poisoned land had been insured—no harm, no foul;
Besides, it isn't our patch; let the death-brew take it all.

Now, we who spend a far-off time within a distant land
(We took it from the natives, who just didn't understand)
Once found our God as small and weak as sleepy little Gwion;
He came to us a Jew, but we have made him European.

We asked a God to bless *our* crops, but He saw *all* were fed;
We asked a God Who howled for blood, and not for One who bled;
A God Who'd keep our nation pure—but He embraced the stranger.
So, seeing it was Him or us; we summoned the Shape-Changer.

3. Old Welsh: "How his brow shines!"

With optics, buzzwords, focus groups, we looked God in the eyes;
With talking points and Twitter posts, we cut Him down to size;
We can't abide *judge not, give all,* and *love your enemies;*
So we brought the great Shape-Changer to bring *that* God to His
    knees.

So now our God has shifted shape; He brandishes a rifle,
Patrols the border, waves the flag, and legislates a trifle.
With tax-collecting sinners He no more sits down to mirth,
And He's blessed our leaking cauldrons that are poisoning the earth.

And should He rise against as another Taliesin,
From Sandy Hook, Uvalde, or the Colorado Basin,
We'll raise our whistles to our lips, call up the Hounds of Fear,
And we'll be safe from Commies, or whatever's bad that year.

CLEANSING THE TEMPLE

He watched the merchants fleece the pilgrim crowd.
The teachers said that all coins with a face
Were idols, so you could not be allowed
To bring them to the Temple. But the place
To change them was right here! Then buy your doves
For sacrifice in one convenient stop!
The wretched of the earth came up in droves
To purchase expiation in the shop.
The carpenter from Nazareth sat down;
Saw thumbs on every scale, and saw the Law
Exploited with connivance of the crown,
And set his cold plan in the air to thaw.
A fit of passion no prep time affords.
It takes six hours to braid a whip of cords.

THREE SHELTERS

Let's be sure all the rites are done right,
The procedures observed faithfully.
The nuns should discourage the right
To abortion, and let the poor be.
If the priests should abuse any children,
It's not for the lay-folk to whinge.

This is My Son, the Beloved; listen to him.

All the kids should wear Purity Rings,
And sign up for the next mission trip.
Whatever the Praise Leader sings
Must be relevant, heart-felt, and hip.
Do not let gay agendas bewilder
Our youth; the results would be grim!

This is My Son, the Beloved; listen to him.

Do things decently and in order,
In a seemly and dignified way;
Elect an untroublesome warden;
Write a soothing Nativity Play.
Let the ancient traditions be gilded,
Do nothing inspired on a whim.

This is My Son, the Beloved; listen to him.

COFFEE AND SEROQUEL

"I beg your pardon," said the gnat upon the dusty road,
"If I have inconvenienced you by adding, to the load
You carry, my own weight; and all that buzzing 'round your eyes
Could not have helped. For both of these, I do apologize."

The ox said, "What?" and "How's that? Oh, it's you; what did you
    say?"
The gnat again apologized. The ox waved him away,
And said, "Think nothing of it. The fact is, until you spoke,
I hadn't even noticed you. Feel free to use my yoke."

EMRYS MERDDYN[4] AND THE TWO DRAGONS

King Vortigern, to thwart the Saxons, built a castle round;
But every night the fortress would go tumbling to the ground.
His Mages told him, "Find a boy was born without a father;
His blood mix with the mortar, and the castle will stand fast—
Your handiwork will last
Until the Ship of Time has sailed from this shore to the farther.

They found a boy named Emrys, who possessed prophetic sight.
"Why have you brought me here?" he boldly asked both King and
  knight.
"You shall be sacrificed so that my fort will stand aright;
"Your blood shall make the mortar strong that holds my towers aloft!
"Come, boy, now don't be soft;
"Embrace the fate that saves your people from the Saxon blight!"

"Who counseled thus the King?" the boy inquired, nothing daunted.
"My Mages, whose renown for perspicacity is vaunted
"From here to France!" "The law requires an audience with the King
For anyone condemned, to set his case before the throne."
He stood, small and alone.
The court convened to hear what evidence the boy would bring.

"Before I show you everything," the small voice rang, "and more,
I ask your Mages: tell us what is underneath this floor."
The wise men were abashed, because they knew no more than I.

4. English: "Merlin"

"And how was it revealed to you the fort could not be built
"Unless my blood is spilt?"
The Mages stood abashed, confused, unable to reply.

"Bid diggers come," the boy replied; "there is a pool below."
They dug, and quickly found the pool. "Now, surely you must know,"
The boy demanded of the wise, "what lies within this pool?"
When none replied, he said, "There are two jars, joined at the neck."
And when men went to check,
They found Emrys the fatherless was surely no one's fool.

"And what is in these vessels?" Emrys asked. The wise kept still.
"You'll find a silken tent within," he said, and with a thrill,
Attendants pulled the jar apart and found the tent within,
And set it up as in a field before the royal throne.
And when the task was done,
Each courtier felt the gooseflesh rise upon his crawling skin.

"And what is in the tent?" he asked, expecting no reply.
"Two serpents: one of red, and one of white you will espy.
"Observe what happens when the snakes are brought into the light."
The serpents changed to dragons, and upon each other fell,
As fierce as vengeful Hell,
And all stood mute, aghast to see the dragons' awful fight.

Three times the white drove back the red before its fierce advance,
Until the red wyrm rallied, and with new-found strength, it chanced
To hurl the white into the pool whence they'd been drawn, and when
It swam away, gave chase. The hall was silent, moribund,
The courtiers stood stunned,
And trembled, knowing that they stood upon the dragons' den.

"You must build elsewhere," Emrys told the King. "The Saxons fell—
"The white wyrm—shall prevail for now. The red wyrm will expel
"Them at the last, in times far off—but do not think that they
"Will yield without a struggle; they will fight unto the last,
"Lash out, and strike, and blast
"The flowing tide of freedom that begins to rise that day."

The white wyrm meant the Saxons, while the red stood for the Welsh;
But time is a kaleidoscope, revealing something else
In all the various fragments every time we turn the wheel—
In alchemy, red male and white female must be united,
Our separateness requited,
Until we "make the two one," so the universe can heal.

And in this newish world, "white" people dispossessed the "red,"
Until it seemed invasion had left hope-resurgent dead.
Now turn the wheel again, and we can see, with dazzled eyes,
How some claim the supremacy above all other guests—
Their malice is addressed
Toward all the dispossessed, the colorful and marginalized.

Now, the red wyrm has a tale to tell, although the white will brook
No stories of injustice; it will challenge every book
That chronicles the lives of those upon whose backs it built
Its kingdom of oppression; it will silence all the bards,
Break the tablets into shards,
And threaten all the teachers who expose the white wyrm's guilt.

The land of freedom and the home of bravery shall be
A place where courage shuts its mouth, and silent are the free.
For like a cornered animal, the white wyrm will attack
All who cry out for justice, all who speak the truth to power;
But liberty shall flower,
And the dragon red will have its ancient home and freedoms back.

Notes on the Poems

When a poem is in a named traditional form, I have identified the form parenthetically at the end of its note.

WISSAHICKON

Words and Things Swami Vivekananda said that we perceive the world through our five senses, and if we had another sense, we would perceive more things. It often seems to me that words do the opposite; we put a label on something—say, the color green—and we perceive everything we mean by that word with reference to that word. And especially in the spring, the woods are a vast palette of so many tints, tones and shades that I would despair of finding names for them all. Yet once our minds have labelled them all as "green," it becomes so easy not to notice how many colors we are actually seeing.

Invocation The first verse is adapted from the second chapter of the extra-canonical Book of Jubilees. Shawn Sanford Beck brought this book to my attention in his book, *Christian Animism* (Christian Alternative, May 29, 2015). This verse, as well as the epigram from the Gospel of Thomas, are meant to establish a vision of an in-spirited natural world. As a Third Order Franciscan, I had long thought that Francis's habit of addressing fire, water, the earth, the sun, and all creatures as his "brothers" and "sisters" was a mere poetic conceit. But the more I study, the more I come to believe that this was actually his worldview: that our non-human fellow creatures are spiritual beings, too. This is the foundation of my approach to the poems in this book.

What Our Eyes Did This poem owes much to Martin Heidegger's "Essay Concerning Technology," which posits the idea that the human gaze transforms everything from "being-in-itself" to "standing-in-reserve"—that is, we objectify all of creation, seeing the world purely as potential means to human ends. (English Ode)

Stone Speaks Continuing the animistic theme of an in-spirited world, I've attempted to understand the nature of the spirit of stone. When a stone is broken, you have more stones; some stones are composed of one substance, whilst others are an amalgam of various minerals. The nearest simile I could arrive at was the Christian Eucharist, in which Christ is said to be fully present in each broken fragment of bread; each communicant receives, not a fragment of Christ, but the whole. The verse, "We who are many are one body, for we all share in the one bread" (1 Corinthians 10:17) appears in the Communion service, and it seemed the best way of understanding the spiritual essence of stone, both in its mixed-mineral rock state, and in its individual constituent minerals.

The form, which may resemble free verse at first glance, is actually derived from ancient Hebrew poetry, most familiar to many through the psalms and prophetic writings of the Hebrew bible. Rather than being organized by rhyme and meter as Greco-Roman poetry was, or by alliteration as was Teutonic verse, ancient Hebrew poetry was built on pairs of comparable or contrasting ideas.

> *The heavens declare the glory of God,*
> *and the firmament shows his handiwork*
> *One day tells its tale to another,*
> *and one night imparts knowledge to another...*
> *Their sound has gone out into all lands,*
> *and their message to the ends of the world.*
> (Psalm 19, 1–2,4)[5]

Credit to Goodwin, Bruce K. *Guidebook to the Geology of the Philadelphia Area* (Pennsylvania Geological Survey, 1964).

5. Book of Common Prayer, Church Publishing, 1979.

The Fox and the Goose A little drama I saw unfold at the Morris Arboretum, from a vantage point on the trail that follows the Wissahickon. (English Ode)

Jewelweed Speaks Interestingly, the sap of the jewelweed is a fine remedy for stinging nettle. Even more interestingly, jewelweed tends to grow right in the same places as stinging nettle. So it probably knows all about healing. (Free verse)

White-tailed Deer Speaks Walking with me along Cresheim Creek—a tributary of the Wissahickon that empties into Devil's Pool—my dog, Murphy, found a deer skull. As he trotted proudly along the trail with his prize, we made eye contact with three white-tails browsing on a rise above us. "Well, this is awkward," I said to Murph. Neither dog nor deer seemed impressed. Apologies to Hozier. (Sonnet)

The Haunted Mill The people and events in this ballad are all real, with the exception of the firebug ghost, which is, as far as you know, my own invention. (Ballad)

The Fallen Tree This poem takes its valedictory tone from W.B. Yeats's "The Tower."

Golden Retriever Ponders the Impermanence of All Things This poem first appeared in my book, *The Way In: What a Hospice Chaplain Learned Living with Parkinson's, in Poetry and Prose*. That was a mistake. It should have made its debut here. Sorry. (Sonnet)

Gullywasher I made this one up in my head whilst driving through a thunderstorm to a friend's house in Germantown for lunch. We really needed rain and I would have loved to exhort the storm to "Lave the drouths," but Walt Whitman beat me to it.

Maxims of the Trees This piece is my attempt at a *haibun,* a form invented by Japanese poet Matsuo Basho (1644–1694), who wrote *The Narrow Road to the Deep North*. Essentially a prose travelogue, it is liberally punctuated with *haiku* and, in one chapter, *haikai no renga,* a collaborative form in which one poet writes a *haiku,* and the second unpacks its metaphor in a *renga,* comprising two lines of seven syllables each. (The resultant poem of five lines is a *tanka,* the form of the poem "Bitternut Hickory Speaks.") My *haibun*, rather than chronicling a single journey, comprises accounts of several walks in various places within the Wissahickon park system, and one in Carpenter's Woods in Philadelphia's Mount Airy neighborhood.

I am indebted to Dana O'Driscoll's *A Magical Compendium of Eastern North American Trees: Ecology. History, Lore, and Divination* (The Druid's Garden LLC, 2022), and to the Tree of the Week YouTube videos from the University of Kentucky's Forestry and Natural Resources Extension.

- White Ash Speaks. In his book "On the Soul," Aristotle coined the word *entelecheia*, "being-at-work-staying-itself." (See page 9 of *Aristotle's On the Soul and On Memory and Recollection,* translated by Joe Sachs. Green Lion Press, 2001.) The idea that things can be called "real" only to the extent that they have duration, I borrowed from Augustine.

- Bitternut Hickory Speaks (Tanka)

- The Light-bearer Speaks (American Holly). This poem was first published in Druid's Book of Ceremonies, Prayers, and Songs, Volume 2. (Ancient Order of Druids in America, 2023.) (Sonnet)

- Northern Pin-Oak Speaks. The form of this poem is flagrantly modeled after the song "You'll Be Back" from the musical *Hamilton*, by Lin-Manuel Miranda. Sorry.

- American Beech Speaks. A poem about forest succession and the loneliness of being ahead of one's time.

- Honeycomb Coral Slime Mold Speaks. My mother used to love to drive from our home in Syracuse, NY to her childhood home in Bloomsburg, PA, especially in the fall. Her rhapsodies on the beauty of the foliage were borderline embarrassing to my brother and me.

- Unnamed Haiku. Don't let anyone tell you haiku are easy.

Creek Blessing My account of a Winter Solstice ritual developed by the Ancient Order of Druids in America. (Sonnet)

Cherry Blossoms Like Washington DC, Philadelphia has its cherry-blossom time, when the streets, gardens and arboretums are ablaze with gorgeous pink or white blossoming trees. In the the gathering dusk of a hazy March day, however, I saw a blossoming cherry tree in the woods, framed against a darkening sky, and oddly contrasting with the pale green of the understory. It gave me a frisson of weird.

Hermit's Cave Really more a meditation on the mission of Johannes Kelpius and the Monks of the Wissahickon than on the unprepossessing hole in which he meditated. (Psalm)

Devil's Pool There are—not so much actual stories, as vague references to hypothetical stories—about Devil's Pool, which generally have to do with the Lenapé "good spirit" imprisoning the "evil spirit" there. Having searched and searched unsuccessfully for an actual story to this effect, I have concluded that the whole thing is yet another example of white people mapping their own worldview onto indigenous cosmologies. I have therefore adapted the Lenapé story of the "Lost Boy" (as told in *The White Deer* by John Bierhorst, William Morrow and Company, 1995) as a poem, as being more in keeping with the Lenapé worldview as I understand it.

Although I have been as faithful as practicable to the original story, I did move the big reveal from the mouth of the Delaware to the confluence of the Delaware and the Schuylkill, being unable to imagine people from the Wissahickon Gorge area traveling all the way to the mouth of the Delaware en masse overnight. Besides, the Lenapé name for the Schuylkill is *Gonshowahanna*, meaning "great, roaring river," and I couldn't possibly not use a word as cool as that. And yes, I am fully alive to the irony of the fact that, in order to write a Lenapé poem to replace a European fantasy, I had to borrow from the Rape of Persephone and the biblical Letter to the Hebrews.

I showed this poem to Adam Waterbear DePaul, Storykeeper of the Lenapé Nation of Pennsylvania, who made some suggestions

that led to some small revisions. I am also indebted to http://www.
native-languages.org/lenape-legends.htm a trove of information
on Lenapé language and lore. (Psalm)

Falling Off a Log True story. (Sonnet)

Crossing the Creek I'm tempted not to tell you what this poem
is "about," because no one I have heard comment on it ever men-
tioned the theme I had in mind. But I will anyway.

Crossing the creek is a metaphor for death, whilst returning
is a metaphor for rebirth. But if you read it a different way, I'm sure
you're right. Poems, like children, leave home and interact with all
kinds of people we don't know. (Sonnet)

the end (Haiku)

OTHER POEMS

The Truth from Below Modeled on the English folk-carol, "The
Truth From Above," this poem may be sung to the same tune.

My argument here is, technically, specious. The New Testa-
ment contains two Greek words both translated as "flesh": *sarx* and
soma. The latter, which appears only once or twice in the whole
Greek bible, means the physical body. The former, which Paul uses
exclusively in his letters, refers to "the carnal nature."

Since the whole Christ enterprise is founded on God taking
on human flesh, it doesn't follow that "the sins of the flesh" spring
primarily from the human body itself. Jesus seems to have liked
to eat and drink (Matthew 11:19) and spent a lot of his ministry
making sure others could do the same (Matthew 14:13–21, et al.)
His first miracle was turning +/-100 gallons of water, set apart for
ritual ablutions, into wine for a wedding feast (John 2:1–11), and
he allowed himself to be anointed with a year's wages worth of oil
of nard (John 12:3). When Paul wrote "make no provision for the
flesh, to gratify its desires" (Roman 13:14, ESV), he used the word
sarx, meaning the debased carnal nature.

Nevertheless, so many Christians are ignorant of this distinction, and the churches have done such a poor job of explaining it, that many non-Christians are justified in thinking Christians "hate the body." It is on this basis that I have called out, if not Paul himself, Christians who misapply his teaching. This poem first appeared on Earth and Altar (earthandaltarmag.com).

If There Were No Such Thing as Food I owe the central conceit of this poem to Thomas Aquinas's "Argument from Desire," as set forth in his *Summa Contra Gentiles:*

> *It is impossible for natural desire to be empty, for nature does nothing in vain. Now, a natural desire would be in vain if it could never be fulfilled. Therefore, man's natural desire [for a final happiness proper to his nature] is capable of fulfillment.*

This argument, in turn, has its roots in Aristotle's dictum, "Nature does nothing in vain." *(Physics)* (Sonnet)

Taliesin I am indebted to Damh the Bard's song, "Ceridwen and Taliesin" *(Antlered Crown and Standing Stone,* 2017*)*, for introducing me to this story. It can also be found in the *Mabinogion,* a collection of Welsh tales of the 11th–13th centuries. This poem first appeared at Earth and Altar (earthandaltarmag.com).

Cleansing the Temple I read a comment on a blog post about this New Testament story, as it appears in John 2:12–25, in which Jesus twists or braids a whip of cords before driving the merchants and money-changers out of the Temple. The commenter, a rancher with experience braiding whips, said that it takes about an hour to craft a foot of whip. I have assumed a six-foot whip here, but even if it were shorter, the fact that the process is so time-consuming strongly implies that Jesus' action was premeditated, and not a spontaneous act of passion as it is often portrayed. This poem first appeared at Earth and Altar (earthandaltarmag.com). (Sonnet)

Three Shelters In which the poet mocks Roman Catholics, Evangelicals, and Episcopalians with words from the story of the

Transfiguration of Christ (as it appears in Matthew 17:1–6). This poem is too snarky to have previously appeared anywhere.

Coffee and Seroquel Chronicling my vain attempts to counter Seroquel-induced torpor with caffeine, this allegorical poem is based on a story attributed to Aesop. Interestingly, Chapter 20 of the extra-canonical Book of Enoch lists seven Archangels, rather than the usual four; number six is Saraqâel, "who is over the spirits of the children of men who induce the spirits to sin." Some pharma marketing person dug impressively deep, there.

Emrys Merddyn and the Two Dragons A verse retelling of an old Welsh tale, with a nod to modernity at the end.